THE ROCK 'N' ROLL OLDIES

Car Songbook

Compiled by
Gary Delfiner

RUNNING PRESS
Philadelphia, Pennsylvania

Canadian representatives: General Publishing Co., Ltd., 30 Lesmill Road, Don Mills, Ontario M3B 2T6. International representatives: Worldwide Media Services, Inc., 115 East 23rd Street, New York, NY 10010.

ISBN 0-89471-566-6 (paper)
ISBN 0-89471-567-4 (library binding)
ISBN 0-89471-568-2 (package)

This book may be ordered by mail from the publisher. Please include $1.00 postage. **But try your bookstore first!** Running Press Book Publishers, 125 South 22nd Street, Philadelphia, PA 19103.

Cover design by Toby Schmidt
Cover illustration by Tony Mascio
Interior photographs: Michael Ochs Archives/
    Venice, CA
Typography: Caxton by Just Your Type,
    Philadelphia, PA
    Futura Demi Bold Script by Letraset
Printed by South Sea International, Ltd., Hong Kong

This is dedicated to the "ones" I love—
My mother and father,
Lonnie, Mindy, Sammie, Adam

Contents

Acknowledgments

Jerry and Sylvia Delfiner, my original backers

Larry and Buz Teacher, who share my
love for the music

Harvey Holiday, my friend whose picture is
in the dictionary under "Oldies"

Val Shively, who does his part to keep
rock 'n' roll alive

Al Feilech of B.M.I.

Joan Perri of A.S.C.A.P.

Jay Morganstern of Warner Bros. Publications

Helene Blue of The Goodman Group

Peter Wright of Chappell/Intersong

Mary Bultman of Hal Leonard
Publishing Corporation

Cecile Russo of Southern Music Publishing

Carol Russo of Warner Bros. Publications

Chuck Dabagian of Val Shively Records

Sharon Tendler, who loves the music

The Melnicks, who will always be
in my heart

All the great oldies groups whose music is
still the only true rock 'n' roll

Hank Bezark, without whom those record
hops could never have happened

Note to Singers

The songs in this book are based on the lyrics as they were originally written. In the true spirit of rock 'n' roll, many of the artists improvised when recording them.

Have fun with your own improvisations and remember—rock 'n' roll will never die!

Book of Love

The Monotones

Tell me, tell me, tell me,
Oh, who wrote the Book of Love?
I've got to know the answer,
Was it someone from above?

I wonder, wonder who, who,
Who wrote the Book of Love?

I love you, darling,
Baby, you know I do,
But I've got to see this Book of Love,
Find out why it's true;

I wonder, wonder who, who,
Who wrote the Book of Love?

Chapter One says to love her,
To love her with all your heart,
Chapter Two you tell her
You're never, never, never, ever gonna part.
In Chapter Three remember
The meaning of romance,
In Chapter Four you break up,
But you give her just one more chance.

I wonder, wonder who, who,
Who wrote the Book of Love?

Baby, baby, baby,
I love you, yes, I do;
Well, it says so in this Book of Love,
Ours is the one that's true.

I wonder, wonder who, who,
Who wrote the Book of Love?

Chapter One says to love her,
To love her with all your heart,
Chapter Two you tell her
You're never, never, never, ever gonna part.
In Chapter Three remember
The meaning of romance,
In Chapter Four you break up,
But you give her just one more chance

I wonder, wonder who, who,
Who wrote the Book of Love?

Baby, baby, baby,
I love you, yes, I do;
Well, it says so in this Book of Love,
Ours is the one that's true.

I wonder, wonder who, who,
Who wrote the Book of Love?

Silhouettes

Took a walk and passed your house
Late last night.
All the shades were pulled and drawn
'Way down tight,
From within a dim light cast
  two silhouettes on the shade,
Oh what a lovely couple they made.

Put [his/her] arms around your waist,
Held you tight,
Kisses I could almost taste
In the night,
Wondered why I'm not the [guy/girl]
  whose silhouette's on the shade

I couldn't hide the tears in my eyes
(Ahhh)

Lost control, and rang your bell,
I was sore,
"Let me in, or else I'll beat
Down your door."
When two strangers, who had been
two silhouettes on the shade
Said to my shock "You're on the wrong
block."

Rushed down to your house with wings
On my feet,
Loved you like I've never loved
You my sweet,
Vowed that you and I would be
two silhouettes on the shade
All of our days, two silhouettes
on the shade.

The Rays

Ben E. King

When the night has come
And the land is dark
And the moon is the only
    light we'll see,
No I won't be afraid,
No I won't be afraid
Just as long as you stand,
    stand by me

So, darling, darling,
Stand by me,
Oh, stand by me,
Oh stand,
Stand by me,
Stand by me.

If the sea that we look upon
Should tumble and fall
Or the mountain should
    crumble in the sea,

Stand By Me

I won't cry,
I won't cry,
No I won't shed a tear
Just as long as you stand,
    stand by me.

  Repeat several times:
So, darling, darling,
Stand by me,
Oh, stand by me,
Oh stand,
Stand by me,
Stand by me.

In the Still of the Night

In the still of the night
I held you, held you tight,
'Cause I love, love you so
Promise I'll never let you go
In the still of the night

I remember that night in May;
The stars were bright above
I'll hope
And I'll pray
To keep
Your precious love

Well, before the light
Hold me again with all of
    your might
In the still of the night.

Well, before the light
Hold me again with all of
    your might
In the still of the night.

The 5 Satins

The Skyliners

Since I Don't Have You

 don't have plans and schemes
And I don't have hopes and dreams,
I don't have anything
Since I don't have you.

I don't have fond desires
And I don't have happy hours,
I don't have anything
Since I don't have you.

I don't have happiness and I guess
I never will ever again;
When you walked out on me
In walked the misery
And he's been here since then.

Now I don't have much to share,
And I don't have one to care,
I don't have anything
Since I don't have you you you you
    you you you you you you you you you

What's Your Name?

What's your name?
I have seen you before
What's your name?
May I walk you to the door?
It's so hard to find a
    personality with charms
    like yours for me
Ooh, ooh ooh-ee

What's your name?
Is it Mary or Sue?
What's your name?
Do I stand a chance with you?
It's so hard to find a
    personality with charms
    like yours for me
Ooh-ee, ooh-ee, ooh-ee

Don & Juan

I stood on this corner
Waiting for you to come
    along
So my heart could feel
    satisfied
So please let me be your
    number one
Under the moon,
Under the stars and
    under the sun

What's your name?
Is it Mary or Sue?
What's your name?
Do I stand a chance
    with you?
It's so hard to find a
    personality with charms
    like yours for me
Ooh-ee, ooh-ee, ooh-ee

19

Dion

Here's my story, it's sad but true;
It's about a girl that I once knew.
She took my love then ran around
With ev'ry single guy in town.

Hayp hayp bum-da hady hady, hayp hayp
Bum-da hady hady, hayp hayp
Bum-da hady hady hayp hayp (ahh)

Hayp hayp bum-da hady hady, hayp hayp
Bum-da hady hady, hayp hayp
Bum-da hady hady hayp hayp (ahh)

I should have known it from the very start,
This girl will leave me with a broken heart.
Now listen people what I'm telling you
A-keep away from a Runaround Sue.

Runaround Sue

I miss her lips and the smile on her face,
The touch of her hair and this girl's
   warm embrace.
So if you don't wanna cry like I do
A-keep away from a Runaround Sue.

Hayp hayp bum-da hady hady, hayp hayp
Bum-da hady hady, hayp hayp
Bum-da hady hady hayp hayp (ahh)

She likes to travel around
She'll love you but she'll put you down.
Now people let me put you wise,
Sue goes out with other guys.

Here's the moral and the story from the
   guy who knows,
I fell in love and my love still grows.
Ask any fool that she ever knew
They'll say keep away from a
   Runaround Sue.

Hayp hayp bum-da hady hady, hayp hayp
Bum-da hady hady, hayp hayp
Bum-da hady hady hayp hayp (ahh)

She likes to travel around
She'll love you but she'll put you down.

(Continued)

Now people let me put you wise,
Sue goes out with other guys.

Here's the moral and the story from the
        guy who knows,
I fell in love and my love still grows.
Ask any fool that she ever knew
They'll say keep away from a
        Runaround Sue.

Hayp hayp bum-da hady hady, hayp hayp
Bum-da hady hady, hayp hayp
Bum-da hady hady hayp hayp (ahh)

Frankie Lymon and the Teenagers

22

Why Do Fools Fall in Love?

Oo-wah, oo-wah
Oo-wah, oo-wah
Oo-wah, oo-wah

Why do fools fall in love?

Why do birds sing so gay
And lovers await the break
    of day?
Why do they fall in love?

Why does the rain fall
    from up above
Why do fools fall in love?

Why do they fall in love?

Love is a losing game
Love can be a shame
I know of a fool, you see
For that fool is me

Tell me why
Tell me why

Why do birds sing so gay
And lovers await the break
    of day?
Why do they fall in love?

Why does the rain fall
    from up above
Why do fools fall in love?
Why do they fall in love?

Why does my heart
Skip a crazy beat?
For I know
It will reach defeat

Tell me why
Tell me why

Why do fools fall in love?

Shep and the Limelights

Daddy's Home

You're my love, you're my angel,
You're the girl of my dreams.
I'd like to thank you
for waiting patiently.

Daddy's home,
Daddy's home to stay.

How I waited for this moment
To be by your side!
Your best friend's around and told me
You had teardrops in your eyes.

Daddy's home,
Daddy's home to stay.

It wasn't on a Sunday,
Monday and Tuesday went by.
It wasn't on a Tuesday afternoon.
All I could do was cry.

But I made a promise that you treasure,
I made it back all to you.

How I waited for this moment
To be by your side!
Your best friend's around and told me
You had teardrops in your eyes.

Daddy's home,
Daddy's home to stay.

Up On the Roof

When this old world starts a-getting me down
And people are just too much for me to face,
I'll climb 'way up to the top of the stairs
And all my cares just drift right into space.

On the roof it's peaceful as can be
And there the world below don't bother me.

So when I come home feeling tired and beat,
I'll go up where the air is fresh and sweet.
I'll get far away from the hustling crowd
And all that rat-race noise down in
    the street.

The Drifters

On the roof that's the only place I know
Where you just have to wish to make it so,
Up on the roof.

At night the stars put on a show for free
And, darling, you can share it all with me.

(I keep a-tellin' you) right smack dab in
     the middle of town
I found a paradise that's trouble-proof
And if this world starts getting you down,
There's room enough for two up on the roof.

Little Anthony and the Imperials

Tears On My Pillow

You don't remember me
But I remember you
'Twas not so long ago
You broke my heart in two
Tears on my pillow
Pain in my heart
Caused by you.

If we could start anew
I wouldn't hesitate
I'd gladly take you back
And tempt the hand of fate

Tears on my pillow

Pain in my heart
Caused by you
Hoo-hoo-hoo-hoo-hoo.

Love is not a gadget
Love is not a toy
When you find the one you
still love [she'll/he'll] fill
your heart with joy

If we could start anew
I wouldn't hesitate
I'd gladly take you back
And tempt the hand of fate

Tears on my pillow
Pain in my heart
Caused by you.

(Optional verse:)
Before you go away
My darling think of me
There may be still a chance
To end this misery.

Tears on my pillow
Pain in my heart
Caused by you.

Duke of Earl

s I walk through this world,
Nothing can stop the Duke of Earl,
And you are my girl,
And no one can hurt you,

Yes I'm gonna love you
Let me hold you,
'Cause I'm the Duke of Earl.

When I hold you,
You will be the Duchess of Earl,

When I walk through my Dukedom,
The paradise we will share,

I'm gonna love you
Let me hold you,
'Cause I'm the Duke of Earl.

I'm gonna love you
Let me hold you,
'Cause I'm the Duke of Earl.

Gene Chandler

31

The Flamingos

I Only Have Eyes for You

y love must be a kind of blind love;
I can't see anyone but you.

Are the stars out tonight?
I don't know if it's cloudy or bright.

I only have eyes for you, dear.

The moon may be high,
But I can't see a thing in the sky,

'Cause I only have eyes for you.

I don't know if we're in a garden
Or on a crowded avenue.

You are here, so am I.
Maybe millions of people go by,
But they all disappear from view,

And I only have eyes for you.

Donna

h Donna, Oh Donna
Oh Donna, Oh Donna

I had a girl,
Donna was her name
Since she's been gone,
I've never been the same.
'Cause I love my girl
Donna, where can you be?
Where can you be?

Now that you're gone
I'm left all alone,
All by myself
To wander and roam;
How I love my girl,
Donna, where can you be?
Where can you be?

Well, Donna,
Now that you're gone

I don't know what I'll do.
All the time and all my love
For you, just for you.

I had a girl,
Donna was her name
Since she's been gone,
I've never been the same.
'Cause I love my girl
Donna, where can you be?
Where can you be?

Oh Donna, Oh Donna
Oh Donna, Oh

Ritchie Valens

The Shirelles

Will You Love Me Tomorrow?

Tonight you're mine completely,
You give your love so sweetly;
Tonight the light of love is in your eyes.
Will you still love me tomorrow?

Is this a lasting treasure,
Or just a moment's pleasure?
Can I believe the magic of your sigh?
Will you still love me tomorrow?

Tonight with words unspoken,
You say that I'm the only one,

But will my heart be broken
When the night meets the morning sun?

I'd like to know that your love
Is love I can be sure of.
So tell me now and I won't ask again.
Will you still love me tomorrow?

So tell me now and I won't ask again.
Will you still love me tomorrow?
Will you still love me tomorrow?

Sixteen Candles

Sixteen candles
Make a lovely sight
But not as bright
As your eyes tonight.

Blow out the candles
Make your wish come true
For I'll be wishing
That you love me too

You're only sixteen
But you're my teenage queen
You're the prettiest,
    loveliest girl I've ever seen

Sixteen candles
In my heart will glow
For ever and ever
For I love you so

You're only sixteen
But you're my teenage queen
You're the prettiest,
    loveliest girl I've ever seen

Sixteen candles
In my heart will glow
For ever and ever
For I love you so

The Crests